# SHE STILL HERE

# She Still Here

GWENDOLYN JACKSON

# Contents

*Dedication*   vii
*Acknowledgements*   ix
*Foreword*   xi
*Introduction*   xiii

1. The First Sign — 1
2. The Diagnosis — 2
3. Starting Treatment — 4
4. The Strokes and Heart Attacks — 6
5. Losing Everything — 8
6. Permanently Disabled — 11
7. Cancer Free — 13
8. After Survival : Learning to Live Again — 15
9. Letter to the Woman I was Before Cancer — 17

Copyright © 2025 by Gwendolyn Jackson
All rights reserved. No part of this book may be reproduced in any manner whatsoever without written permission except in the case of brief quotations embodied in critical articles and reviews.
Roy L. Jackson Foundation, 2025

I like to dedicate this book to God, the author of my life, my brother John, my mother, My Kids ( Darian, Eric, and Danielle), my grandchildren (Arianna, Erin, Giannis, and Harmony), and my First Love, My Father, The Late Roy L Jackson. To everyone who has ever felt broken and kept going - this is for you. To the fighters, the survivors, the Caregivers, the dreamers, and the believers. May you find strength in your story and faith in healing.

# Acknowledgements

Writing this book has been one of the most personal journeys of my life. I want to thank the incredible doctors and nurses who cared for me with compassion and skill.

To my family and friends, who lifted me when I could not stand.

To the strangers who offered kindness in unexpected places.

And most of all, to God - for healing me and giving me the courage to keep fighting, and share my story.

# Foreword

In a world that often feels overwhelming, some individuals shine brightly, offering their light to others even in the darkest of times. Gwen Jackson is one such person. Long before the words "cancer diagnosis" ever graced her life, Gwen was a beacon of hope and compassion in her community. She never shied away from the call to action, tirelessly fundraising and organizing relief efforts whenever a natural disaster struck nearby. For years, she has championed the backpack drive, ensuring that children in need have the supplies they require for a successful school year.

Then came the news that shocked us all. Despite her unwavering spirit and contagious energy, Gwen was diagnosed with cancer. Yet, in what could have been a moment of surrender, she chose to fight back with the same tenacity that defined her life. She continued her mission of helping others while confronting her own battle, a testament to her incredible strength and resilience. It was as if she remained untouched by her diagnosis, still giving her all to the causes she held dear.

In this book, Gwen opens up about her journey, inviting us into her world as she navigates the tumultuous waters of illness while holding fast to her core belief: that she exists not just for herself, but for everyone around her. "She Still Here" is not only about the brutal realities of cancer, but also about understanding the importance of faith and determination in times of profound despair. It is okay to prioritize oneself for the first time and to transform that experience into a source of strength for others.

Through her words, readers will find inspiration in their own struggles and the courage to confront their pain. "She Still Here" is a powerful memoir that resonates across all walks of life, encouraging us to embrace our scars and share our stories. Gwen's journey is proof that even in the face of life's greatest challenges, we can rise, we can thrive, and we can extend our hand to lift others along the way.

So, let this book be a light in your life, a reminder that you are not alone in your struggles, and that, like Gwen, you can say too, "I am still here."

By: Valencia N. Lee

# Introduction

**When Everything Changed**

I never imagined my life would shift so violently, so quickly. One moment, I was working, loving, dreaming- and the next, I was unraveling. Diagnosed with cervical cancer that had already started its silent creep into my bones, my world stopped. But life didn't. It kept moving, even as mines fell apart piece by piece.

Before the diagnosis, I thought I had control over my health, my relationships, and my future. Then came the strokes, the heart attacks, the dehydration that nearly ended me, the resignation from the job I loved, the loss of my townhouse, my car, and the man I thought would be by my side through anything. Still, the hits kept coming, but here's the part I never expected: I made it.

This is not just a story about sickness. It's a story about faith. Trusting God with every part of my life. The freedom to be real, to fall apart, to get back up, and to tell the truth. I am now cancer-free, but the scars are both visible and invisible- they tell the story of Faith over Fear.

***XIV  ~  INTRODUCTION***

Writing this book has been one of the most personal journeys of my life. I want to thank the incredible doctors and nurses who cared for me with compassion and skill.

To my family and friends, who lifted me when I could not stand.

To the strangers who offered kindness in unexpected places. And most of all, to God - for healing me and giving me the courage to keep fighting, and share my story.

To everyone who has ever felt broken and kept going - this is for you. To the fighters, the survivors, the Caregivers, the dreamers, and the believers. May you find strength in your story and faith in healing.

When the words came out of the doctor's mouth, I didn't know whether to cry or scream. "You are now considered permanently disabled." It felt like another loss. Another version of myself, buried permanently. That word cut deeper than any diagnosis. Cancer had come to fight. Disability felt like a sentence. It wasn't temporary. It wasn't "until you recover." It was forever.

At first, I rejected it. I told myself I'd bounce back. I'd find a new job, get stronger, and be who I used to be. But my didn't cooperate. The strokes had taken part of my memory. The heart attacks left me with fatigue that never seemed to lift. The radiation had damaged more than the cancer. And the mental weight- depression, anxiety, trauma- was just as disabling as the physical.

No one prepares you for what it feels like when your body becomes a barrier. When just walking to the bathroom feels like a chore. When grocery stores feel like obstacle courses. When you have to fill out forms that say: "unable to work," "requires assistance, " "100% disabled." I looked at those boxes, checked them, and felt my worth drain. Who was I now, if I couldn't work? If I couldn't drive? If I couldn't keep up with the world moving at full speed while I was stuck in slow motion?

For a while, I felt useless. There were days I didn't want to talk to anyone. I isolated myself because I didn't want people to see me like this - struggling, tired, and dependent. I felt like I had to constantly explain myself. Justify my pain. Prove my limitations. And the paperwork. The phone calls. The government systems that don't see people but only numbers. Being told I had to " prove" my condition. I was questioned about how sick I was. As if surviving wasn't enough evidence.

But in the silence of those hard days, I started to realize something: Disabled doesn't mean defeated. It means changed. It means I live differently now. It means I carry more than most, and still rise.

Yes, I am disabled. But I am also a survivor. A woman who has stared death in the face and said, "Not today." I may need to rest more than others. I may move slower. But my life still matters. My voice still Matters. Being declared disabled wasn't the end of my Story. It was the beginning of reclaiming it.

I started seeing my strength in new ways- not in how much I could do, but in how I kept showing up! I gave myself permission to grieve the life I lost while also embracing the life I still had.

## XVI ~ INTRODUCTION

And slowly, I began to rebuild. Not into the woman I was before- but into someone braver. Someone who had already survived the unimaginable... and was still standing.

# Chapter 1

# The First Sign

It didn't start with something dramatic. No collapsed lungs or sudden fainting spells- just a persistent pain. A nagging discomfort in my pelvic area that I tried to ignore. I'd just had my well-woman exam, and things were chaotic due to COVID.

For weeks, I told myself it was just my fibroid. But deep down, something felt off. My body was whispering to me, and I wasn't listening. Suddenly, it started screaming!

The fatigue hit next, a bone-deep exhaustion that no amount of sleep could fix.

Then came the bleeding - irregular, painful, and alarming. That's when fear crept in. Quiet at first. Then louder. Still, I hesitated. I kept pushing through workdays, pretending everything was fine. I continued to smile when I was tired. I showed up even when I was breaking down inside.

It wasn't until I started leaking clear fluids one day in the garage after lifting something heavy. I finally went to the emergency room.

That day marked the beginning of everything!

# Chapter 2

# The Diagnosis

Ill never forget the silence in that room. It was the kind of silence that says more than any words ever could.

The doctor looked at me, her eyes soft but serious. The way doctors look when they've rehearsed what they're about to say but still hope they won't have to. She cleared her throat. "There's no easy way to say this," she began." You have cervical cancer."

Everything slowed down. I didn't cry. Not right away. Instead, I sat there, frozen. I was caught somewhere between shock and disbelief. My brain scrambled to make sense of it. Cancer?

That's what happens to other people, I thought. That's what my Dad passed on to my Aunt. I am the CEO/ Founder of a Cancer organization. Not me, I was just tired. Just stressed. I was supposed to bounce back, not break down, but she wasn't finished.

After removing the tumor and starting radiation, the doctor told me, "It's already spread," she said, more quietly this time. Then she continued, "To your bones." Just like that, everything I thought I knew about my life changed. My plans. My job. My future. My body. All of it suddenly felt like it didn't belong to me anymore. The word "metastatic" hit like a punch to the chest. I didn't know much about it then, but I knew enough that no one in my family had survived cancer. What followed next was a blur- referrals, scans, labs, biopsies.

Doctors were speaking in a language that sounded more clinical than human. Words like "aggressive, "invasive," and "treatment-resistant" swirled in my head like a storm I couldn't escape. I held it together until I was alone. Then I broke, I sat sobbing until I couldn't breathe, and when the tears finally stopped, a numbness settled in, not acceptance. Not peace. Just .... emptiness.

I thought of everything at once - my kids, my job, my townhouse, my boyfriend, my family, my independence, and how I was going to fight this and still hold my life together.

The truth was- I couldn't.

What I didn't know in that moment was that this diagnosis was not just the beginning of a battle with cancer- it was the beginning of my true walk with God. One that would strip everything I thought defined me.

## Chapter 3

# Starting Treatment

The word "treatment" sounded hopeful at first. It made me think of healing. Of medicine doing its job. Life getting better. But what they don't tell you - What the pamphlets and polite doctors often leave out is that treatment for cancer doesn't feel like healing.

It feels like war. A quiet, invisible war is happening inside your body while you try to hold on to your mind and your spirit. My treatment plan included radiation five days a week and chemo pills taken at home. No long infusion chairs or IV poles- just little white pills that looked harmless until I swallowed them.

What they really were: poison with a purpose. Radiation was its own kind of hell.

Every morning, I lay on a cold metal table, staring up at a ceiling that never changed. I had to lie perfectly still while a machine rotated around me, burning away cancer cells- and, sometimes, my sense of humanity. The technicians were kind, but everything about the process made me feel like a number. A case file. A body. Not a person. The side effects came fast.

First, the nausea, not just queasy, but a gut-deep sickness that made even the thought of food unbearable. Then the fatigue- not just tired, but empty. Like my bones were made of lead, like my energy had been stolen while I slept. My skin burned. My insides cramped. There were days I couldn't get out of bed, days I didn't recognize myself in the mirror. My hair began to thin. My appetite disappeared. I lost weight. I lost time. I lost pieces of myself. I thought I needed to survive.

The chemo pills were supposed to be "easier" than IV chemo, but there's nothing easy about waking up every day knowing you're about to poison yourself again. My hands would shake before I took them. I'd stare at the bottle, my reflection in the glass of the bathroom mirror reminding me I didn't have a choice.

And still - I showed up. To every session. To every scan. I took every pill with every breath, even when it hurt. Especially when it hurt. Because deep down, I wasn't just fighting for my body- I was fighting for my life. For the chance to keep telling my story. For the hope that one day, the pain would be behind me and not ahead of me, but that hope was fragile.

The world around me kept moving while mine felt like it was breaking apart. Friends didn't understand. My body couldn't keep up. My heart was tired. Yet- I kept going. Not because I always believed I could make it, but because I didn't want to give up before I saw what was on the other side of the storm. I didn't know it yet, but the worst wasn't over. The dehydration, the strokes, the heart attacks, and the heartbreak- they were still coming. But I would survive all of that, too.

# Chapter 4

# The Strokes and Heart Attacks

I didn't know dehydration could kill you.

It started subtly. My mouth was always dry. My skin lost its glow. I felt dizzy more often. It felt like I was walking on uneven ground. But I told myself I was just tired from treatment. I had learned to expect pain, to normalize suffering.

Then I couldn't speak properly. I remember trying to form a sentence, and the words came out broken and out of order. My hands, face, and legs were weak. I had my first TIA - Transient Ischemic Attack, also called a mini-stroke. Then came another. And another. Three in total throughout the year. Each one felt like a warning shot. The doctors told me it was caused by being severely dehydrated.

The dehydration was made worse by the chemotherapy, radiation, and the constant nausea. Drinking water felt like I was swallowing glass. My body was crying out for help, and I hadn't been listening - not because I didn't care, but because I had been in survival mode.

The strokes didn't stop there. Every day was about getting through the next hour. I started having sharp chest pain. It came suddenly. It felt like someone was squeezing my heart with both hands. I was convinced it was stress - until I couldn't catch my breath, so I went to the emergency room.

The Emergency room doctor told me I'd had a mild heart attack. Not long after, a second one. Both were tied to the same root cause: dehydration, stress, and the physical toll of cancer treatment.

My heart was literally breaking under the pressure. I was angry. Angry that no one had warned me this could happen. Angry that my body kept failing when I was trying so hard to fight. Angry that I had done this to myself by not drinking water. Yet... I was still here. That was the part that humbled me. Despite all of it- the strokes, the heart attacks, the days I thought I wouldn't wake up, but I did wake up. I kept waking up. There were nights I slept with fear on my chest, wondering if I'd make it to morning. There were days I was too weak on the left side to walk. Too weak to cry. But there was always something- a whisper inside me- that said, "You're not done yet." That voice was small, but it was enough. That voice helped me start listening to my body in a new way. I learned to slow down. To hydrate. To ask for help, even when I didn't want to.

I learned that healing wasn't just about fighting - it was also about surrendering.

Not to Cancer ... But to God!!!

# Chapter 5

# Losing Everything

They don't tell you that Cancer doesn't just take from your body. It takes from your life.

When people hear, "You have Cancer."

They think about hospitals and medicine. They don't think about eviction notices. Missed paychecks. Losing your car in the middle of treatment. They don't think about how many times you'll have to say, "I'm sorry, I just can't anymore."

But I lived it.

First, it was my job. I tried to hold on. I showed up even when I was sick, even when my legs could barely carry me. I didn't want to let anyone down. I didn't want to let myself down. But eventually, I couldn't fake it anymore. The fatigue, the memory loss from strokes, the emotional weight - I wasn't the same person. I had to resign. Letting go of my career was like losing a part of my identity. I had worked hard. I had pride in what I did. That job was stability, structure- mine, and suddenly, it wasn't.

Then came the car. Without income, I fell behind on payments. I remember handing over the keys and feeling this strange sense of shame, even though I knew it wasn't my fault. But when everything around you is slipping away, guilt finds a way in, even when you've done nothing wrong. Next was the townhouse. The place I called home. The place that held my memories, my comfort, my peace. Gone, I had to leave the space where I once dreamed about the future and learned instead how to survive in the present.

Perhaps most painful of all, I lost the man who I thought loved me. We had been together for seven years. We had history. We had plans. But cancer doesn't just test your body - it tests your relationships. We grew apart in ways I couldn't stop. He needed the old Gwen, and I knew she was gone and would never return. He needed the quick return phone calls. To be prioritized first. But I needed distance. In the end, we couldn't meet in the middle. There was no big fight. Just silence where love used to live. It was heartbreaking. Not just because of the breakup, but I also needed financial security because of bills and treatment. Now I was drowning in debt. Most importantly, I thought I'd never be lovable again. I was losing my hair, my body was scarred, and my energy was gone. I didn't feel beautiful. I didn't feel like myself. I wondered if I'd ever be wanted again, not out of pity- but out of genuine love. But through all of this, I kept waking up.

There were days I screamed into pillows, cried on bathroom floors, questioned God, and begged for a break. I felt invisible. Forgotten. Broken. But I was still breathing. Every breath became proof that even though I had lost so much, I hadn't lost everything. I still had my soul. I still had my will. In the ashes of all I had to let go, I started to find something else: Myself.

Not the version that had it all together. But the version that had been through hell and was still here.

Raw. Real. Resilient, and born again through Christ Jesus.

This was the beginning of the Potter (God) making me over again. But first, I had to accept one hard truth:
I would never go back to who I was.

Maybe.... that was the point.

# Chapter 6

# Permanently Disabled

When the words came out of the doctor's mouth, I didn't know whether to cry or scream. "You are now considered permanently disabled."

It felt like another loss. Another version of myself, buried and permanent. That word cut deeper than any diagnosis. Cancer had come to fight. Disability felt like a sentence. It wasn't temporary. It wasn't "until you recover." It was forever. At first, I rejected it. I told myself I'd bounce back. I'd find a new job, get stronger, and be who I used to be.

But my didn't cooperate. The strokes had taken part of my memory. The heart attacks left me with fatigue that never seemed to lift. The radiation had damaged more than the cancer. And the mental weight- depression, anxiety, trauma- was just as disabling as the physical. No one prepares you for what it feels like when your body becomes a barrier. When just walking to the bathroom feels like a chore. When grocery stores feel like obstacle courses. When you have to fill out forms that say: "unable to work," "requires assistance," and "100% disabled." I looked at those boxes, checked them, and felt my worth drain.

Who was I now, if I couldn't work? If I couldn't drive? If I couldn't keep up with the world moving at full speed while I was stuck in slow motion?

For a while, I felt useless. There were days I didn't want to talk to anyone. I isolated myself because I didn't want people to see me like this - struggling, tired, dependent. I felt like I had to constantly explain myself. Justify my pain. Prove my limitations. And the paperwork. The phone calls. The government systems that don't see people but only numbers. Being told I had to " prove" my condition. I was questioned about how sick I really was. As if surviving wasn't enough evidence. But in the silence of those hard days, I started to realize something: Disabled doesn't mean defeated.

It means changed, it means I live differently now. It means I carry more than most, and still rise. Yes, I am disabled. But I am also a survivor. A woman who has stared death in the face and said, "Not today." I may need to rest more often. I may move more slowly. But my life still matters. My voice still Matters.

Being declared disabled wasn't the end of my story.

It was the beginning of reclaiming it. I started seeing my strength in New ways- not in how much I could do, but in how I kept showing up! I gave myself permission to grieve the life I lost while also embracing the life I still had.

And slowly, I began to rebuild. Not into the woman I was before- but into someone braver. Someone who had already survived the unimaginable... and was still standing.

# Chapter 7

# Cancer Free

I didn't cry at first, I just sat there- stunned, silent, still.

On June 29, 2025, while at The Refreshing Church in Houston, Texas, with Pastor John A. Murray III, his lovely wife, and the church family, I read my scans in my patient portal. I couldn't believe it! The scans read, "Your Scans are clear. There's no evidence of disease."

Those words - " no evidence of disease" should have echoed like music in my ears. But instead they landed softly, like something fragile I was afraid to touch. When you've spent so long surviving, it's hard to believe you're actually safe. I nodded, slowly, like I understood. But inside, my thoughts were swirling. What now? Is it really over? Can I trust this moment? Can I finally breathe?

After years of hospitals, pain, pills, and fear, I expected the finish line to feel different. Bigger. Louder. Brighter. But the truth is, healing doesn't arrive like fireworks. It arrives like a whisper: "You're still here."

When I walked out of that clinic, the sun felt different, warmer, and softer. I stood in the parking lot, looked up at the sky, and let the tears fall. I lifted my hands up to God in total Praise. I cried for everything I had lost. I cried for the version of me that wouldn't return. I cried because I had made it- and I didn't know who I was without the fight.

Being cancer-free wasn't just a celebration. It was a spiritual journey. I had to learn to Trust God. I had to learn to live without fear but with faith. I had to reclaim my body - not as a battleground, but as a home. People expected me to be happy, and I was. But I was also... changed. I was more grateful and more tender with life. The truth is: being cancer-free doesn't erase what you've been through. It doesn't bring back the job, the carp, the townhouse, or the relationship. It doesn't undo the trauma or silence the fear of recurrence. But it gives you something else:

A second chance
A deeper kind of gratitude.
A quiet power that no one can take.

I didn't walk away from cancer as the same woman who walked in. I walked away stronger, softer, wiser- and so deeply aware of every breath I take.

Today, I still live with the echoes of that battle. But the battle doesn't own me. I own this moment. This chapter. This body. This Life. And while cancer may be part of my story, it will never be the end of it.

# Chapter 8

# After Survival : Learning to Live Again

Surviving Cancer is one thing. Learning how to live again - that's something else entirely.

There's no guidebook for what comes after the finish line. No one tells you that healing doesn't stop when the scans come back clear. That's just when a new journey begins. After everything I had been through - diagnosis, treatment strokes, heart attacks, loss upon loss- I expected to feel nothing but joy.

But what I felt was more complicated than that. There was joy, yes. But there was also fear. Guilt. Emptiness. And a big, unanswered question: Who am I now?

I had spent so long in survival mode that it became my identity. Wake up. Take the pills. Go to treatment. Fight—rest. Repeat.

That rhythm- harsh as it was- had structure. Now there was none. Just quiet. And in that quiet, I had to face myself. I didn't have a job to return to. I didn't have my home, my car, or my relationship. I had my body- still recovering. My mind - still healing. And my spirit - bruised but not broken. So I started slow.

I learned how to breathe again without fear in my chest. I began to eat again, not out of obligation, but pleasure. I walked outside and let the sun touch my skin, not because it was part of therapy, but because I wanted to feel alive. I allowed myself to grieve - not just the pain I had endured, but the woman I used to be. I gave myself permission to embrace the woman I was becoming. She was softer. More patient. She valued stillness as much as strength. She didn't care as much about being understood by others - only about being true to herself. Being disabled didn't mean being defeated - it meant finding new ways to thrive.

Being single didn't mean I was unlovable- it meant I had space to rediscover myself without compromise. Being a survivor didn't mean I had to be superhuman- it meant I had broken, rebuilt, and I was still here.

Living again wasn't about " going back to normal." It was about building something entirely new from the ground up, with intention and grace.
Some days I still struggle. Some nights, the fear creeps back in. But most days, I find moments of peace, laughter, and purpose. And in those moments, I remember: I didn't survive just to exist, but I survived to live.

# Chapter 9

# Letter to the Woman I was Before Cancer

Dear Gwen,

I wish I could sit beside you right now, hold your hand, and tell you everything will be okay because I know you're scared. I know you're hurting. I know you feel like your whole world is falling apart.

You don't understand it yet, but this storm you're walking through - it's not the end of your life story. It's the beginning of a new chapter. A chapter that will test you in ways you never imagined, but will also reveal a strength you didn't know you had. I want you to know:

It's okay to be afraid.
It's okay to cry.
It's okay to feel broken.

Because healing isn't about being perfect or strong all the time. It's about showing up, day after day, even when you don't want to. It's about learning to love yourself when the mirror reflects someone you barely recognize.

You will lose things. You will lose parts of your life you thought were yours forever. But you will also find parts of yourself that were hidden, waiting to be discovered. You will learn to be gentle with your body, with your mind, with your heart. You will learn to say no to things that don't serve you and yes to things that bring you peace. You will learn that your worth isn't tied to your job, your relationship, or your independence- it's tied to your spirit. And that spirit- your spirit - is fierce. It is resilient. It is unbreakable.

One day, you will look back and realize how far you've come. You will see the battles you fought, the tears you shed, and the love you gave yourself. And you will be proud. So keep going. Keep breathing. Keep believing. Because the woman you will become- stronger, wiser, kinder - is waiting for you on the other side of this pain.
And she will carry your story with grave and power.

With all my love,

Gwendolyn Jackson